# Extra Pith

Poems and songs by Jesse Kates

Kansas City　Spartan Press　Missouri

**Spartan Press**
Kansas City, Missouri
spartanpresskc.com

Copyright (c) Jesse Kates, 2017
First Edition 1 3 5 7 9 10 8 6 4 2
ISBN: 978-1-946642-21-9
LCCN: 2017947292

Interior design and layout: Jason Ryberg
Author photo: Forester Michael
Cover art, design and layout: Gavin Snider
All rights reserved. No part of this publication may be reproduced or transmitted in any form or by any means, electronic or mechanical, including photocopying, recording or by info retrieval system, without prior written permission from the author.

Prospero's Books and Spartan Press would like to thank Jeanette Powers, j.d.tulloch, Jason Preu, M. Scott Douglass, Shawn Pavey, Shawn Saving, Jesse Kates, Jim Holroyd, Steven H.Bridgens, Thomas Mason, Beth Dille, Mason Wolf, The West Plaza Tomato Co., The Osage Arts Community and The Robert J. Deuser Foundation For Libertarian Studies.

CONTENTS

1 I'll Get Out of Your Hair
2 Reduction in Force
3 Geminids
4 Amaro
6 *Shadow Of Doubt*
7 435 Loop
9 Forest Cathedral
10 Union Station
11 Winter, Columbus Park
12 *I'm Going To Love Your New Boyfriend*
14 Reminders
15 You Can't Always Get What You Want
16 Rhodes Suitcase
17 Smudged Lenses
18 Red Hymnals
19 *You're My All Creation*
20 Quantum Entanglement
21 We Will Make No Distinction
23 Always Sometimes
24 Suspension
25 *Not About Girls*
26 1991
27 Portrait of Lazarus
28 Remember Who You Are
29 Driving Jonas to School
30 Homecoming
31 *Sneaky*
32 Political Agenda
33 *Goats, Biscuits, Bees*
34 Wildlife Observatory

35 Charlene and Manny
36 Raytown Open House
37 *Drill To The Hull*
39 Forecast
40 The Art Teacher
41 Statue of Limitations
42 Seacats
43 Prophet and Loss
44 Betty Moody's Cave
46 *I Need You To Be Real*
48 Christmas Day
50 Mantoloking Redux
52 Ends
53 Stuck Spark
54 *She's The Memory You Keep*
56 Silt
57 84 WPM
58 40 Days, 40 Nights
59 Quick Cuts
60 After the Inauguration
61 Burrs
62 Mid-American Shakespeare
63 Prospectus
64 Art of Not Asking
65 *I Do Or Adieu*
67 Forgiveness
68 *Like Petrichor*
69 Anniversary
70 B7
72 Once in a Lifetime

Thanks

to Carly, Steph, Megan, Will and Jim for the feedback

to Jason and Jeanette for the opportunity

## I'll Get Out of Your Hair

I want my departure
embossed: a kiss, a rise.
You sigh under
blanket knit brown.
Purple hoodie.
White pajama pants.
Phone's blue
lighting your face.

Bright moon.
I lock the deadbolt.

If I hurled this key
glinting to the feral cats,
I'd scale the fence,
crawl the dark wet grass.

Dash guages. Fumbled wire
for tunes.
        In your living room
your feet cross my name
carved in your coffee table.

## Reduction in Force

Parking lot snowbanks smoothed
by wind. Rock salt bleaches
asphalt in waves of white residue.
A vice president slips on black ice,
shoe flashing skyward in perfect
compass curve like flapping arms
of a snow angel, grimy kiss
on his backside just the mark
of a little needed kick in the ass.

                      Layoffs again. Sun
strikes a hard angle. A heel turn
down an aisle vanishes contents
of cubes: dust tufts, push pins,
cracked glass in photo frame,
picture gone. Rows with empties
are slots on a yearbook page:
smile smile blank. Smile smile
blank.

## Geminids

Air and leaves crackle
like ice cubes in hot tea.
Bowl of blueberry sky
spills above. We lie
on car hood.
           Cold creeps
our backs like fingernails.
Our breath mists like starmilk.
We await punctuation of meteors
falling like caresses
                    on a black
sleeve of roadway resting
on a hard table of brittle
grass. Cars pass, comets
blanching landscape
like lighthouse or prison
spot but mittens hide
our eyes.
           We drive in dry
heat, smelling gasoline.
We retreat like stars from sun
to our golden geometry
of asphalt and streetlights
until only Mars glints
above our yard.

## Amaro

*I would marry you
if you left your wife*
she says over amaro's
minty, herbed heat.
I've got a kids' puzzle
with metal marble
tilting in my hands.
Truth is layered
between us delicate
and sweet, a thousand
sheets of phyllo.
We linger past close.
The bar staff joke, comp
our drinks. *Stay the night.
I'll snuggle you,* she invites.
I trace ridges of her house
key in my jacket pocket.

She slips PJs on discreetly
above cold bathroom tiles.
I keep jeans. *No street
clothes,* she says. I breathe
the softness of her neck,
tune to every second
of golden street glow
in sympathetic vibration.
Her cat paws the blinds.

Our arms and legs braid
in warm flannel until 3am.

She shuts 30 Rock from her laptop.

*You're my guy and it's never
going to happen. It's OK,
though.* I kiss her head,
murmur *I'd marry you, too.*

## Shadow Of Doubt

I pull up at home
autumn afternoon
a strange car in the drive
I'm early, dear

the purse in the hall
surely isn't yours
I silently sink in a chair
as your footsteps hit the stairs

I'm waiting for the film to play out
I can't leave under a shadow of doubt

when your mother asked
I said it was a phase
from the dark you call
just to ask me how I've been

on the cobblestones
you're just a pair of girls
as you hold her hand
I want to see how hard you squeeze

I'm waiting for the film to play out
I can't leave under a shadow of doubt

The credits roll
I've got no control
How can I believe this turn?

435 Loop

I am convinced
a man drives
the perimeter
highway all day,
arm arcing the wheel
asphalt turning like a 45
radio rotating voices
drums crashing
like collapsing pot racks
or is it a woman?

Heels, half-eaten
sandwich, empty
child seat, lingering
cigarette, endlessly late
for the same appointment:
show a yellow bungalow
sunken wood porch
cracked lead paint,
rusted propane tank
but where?

I watch to catch her, or him.

Cars stream in lanes
like Hotwheels
on an electric track

held on by a giant
toddler's grip.
White silver tan black
flowing by billboards
for self-storage:
climate controlled,
first month free.

My feet root
papers piled like leaves.

Search for repeats,
skips in the disc:
charts, graphs, logs
pencil shavings, metal
compass you twirled
above lined paper
waiting for the bell.
Handwriting pinches
a cacophony of concert
scores: ticks for make,
model, time, temperature,
shape and feel of clouds.

Eyes to spyglass, a fern
browns on the sill.

Down the hall, water drips.

## Forest Cathedral

Northern Pennsylvania. Air
hushes like empty playground
in snowfall. Old growth pines
arch upward, fading in breath's mist.
My son draped in his mother's hoodie
like a cupcake in purple icing, small
shoes damp with condensation.
Ferns and moss underfoot, colors
vivid as acrylics under a palette
of slate gray cloud.
                In the Midwest, volunteers
shovel hiking trails from overgrowth
of WPA-era park. Bikes and tennis
shoes tamp paths. Occasional piles
of clothes, discarded pizza boxes
and bottles of unknown liquid foster
new growth. Beige and mustard homes
spill like grass seed through fingers,
trees placed like miniatures in display
case smudged by prints.

## Union Station

Distant piano: Silent Night.
Marble floors, walls, ceilings.
A cavern to hangar a zeppelin.
Dangling snowflakes two feet wide.
Fake Christmas trees drip oversize
plastic balls. A bird flutters high,
boxed by an ornamental roof,
lid of accidental habitat. A family
shuffles in matching turquoise jackets,
the scale of parent to child dwarfed
by wreaths huge enough for either
to step through with craned necks
and upturned eyes. Tie dyed shirts
for sale as beyond snowy portholes
salt crusts the chrome of SUVs.
Squeak of heels, skid of stroller
wheels, floor pockmarked and worn
like cow paths leading to water
in hot dirt somewhere. Here, clear
bulbs glaze wood like gingerbread
as the tinkle of silverware diffuses
like the sandy sigh of blowing
snow or the reverberant flap
of small wings as a shadow
darts the floor.

# Winter, Columbus Park

Our loss sucks warmth
like a fish below an ice hole
I sink on bench in bathrobe,
snow crunched by bare toes.
I call across the frozen pond.
Your face lights like a wreath.
You mistake an echo and walk
the wrong way, trailing a leashed
white cat, ragdoll in your arm's
crook. Once your swift gait
lifted our hands to the sun's kiss.
Now a shattered red tree ball
burnishes in icy grass. Like the cat
I am declawed: my only hook to day's
gray cliff my growling stomach.
Please melt this salty rock of lack.
Please silence the absence of bells.

## I'm Going To Love Your New Boyfriend

now I fear I'm doomed
to ricochet around
like that squash ball
you just hammered

you serve up your news
I duck and clench a smile
windows shatter

he's your new boyfriend
you're gonna love him
so I'm gonna love him
'cuz he's your new boyfriend

winter wafting in
when once we were so warm
in a way we're still not speaking

as his hands touch you
I flinch away from harm
oh you're beaming

he's your new boyfriend
you're gonna love him
so I'm gonna love him
'cuz he's your new boyfriend

*at your dinner party*
*our eyes locking as he*
*says he doesn't like Scrabble*
*then he's washing dishes*
*you're laughing from the kitchen*
*my resistance unravels*

## Reminders

don't chop the tops off trees
bury your hatchet in warm butter
no wrist slaps for nail biting boys
eat only Energy Star bulbs
don't drink gravy at salad bars
for late night anxiety, chew foil
only listen to massacres
from the distance of a car radio
when lost in cicada sound
look for the child who cries *moon!*

## You Can't Always Get What You Want

Jonas snuggles my ribs
in backseat as Mick explains
sometimes you eat the sandwich.
Little snotty inhalations: cherry
blossom days. *Why is the sky gray?*
Parenthood is CEO sociopathy:
Ken Lay or Jeff Skilling forcing
the bottom line of a toothbrush
to tiny teeth. But his grasp lingers
longer than the street's crossing.
*You're not in charge of me,* he says,
bursting like a sponge animal
from youth's wet capsule. Easter
potluck, darting a forest of jeans,
Jonas states *I'm tired* and sequesters
in his blue room. At Thanksgiving,
Miracle on 34th's black and white
parade muffled my parents' bickering.
Snow pale, Jonas' asthma puff
accumulation may cost a centimeter
of height. With the stone-washed genes
of his mother's father, never his curls.

## Rhodes Suitcase

En route to Thanksgiving dinner,
my father offers my wife pot candy
like a Canal Street watch salesman.
Sly apéritif. Ticket to distance. He stocks
wine like provisions for a coming storm.
*Five bottles is enough, right?* He swigs
his old self from memory's mottled vodka
bottle. Gray hair roils from his yarmulke
as he detains and interrogates our waitress,
brow furrowed like a sawtooth wave.
Later, for dynamic purposes, he rouses
our black '82 electric piano with the flowing
touch of petite, childlike hands similar to mine.

## Smudged Lenses

My mother's edges
soften. Forgets morning's
argument like magnet
wiping tape. Bulky
shoes black, unscuffed.
She walks Monopoly
dog to Park Place,
waits in tortoise glasses,
unsure. She sends
same email five times,
slightly rearranged. Speech
rehearsal in empty gym.
Lunchbox-size Ziploc
spills sixteen pill bottles.
She wants sugar-free
ice cream. I dream a hike
together, sudden cool.
Shade on an urban trail.

# Red Hymnals

grain of wood pews
sea of murmurs
grey hair, bald sheen
thick braids, red tresses
wreaths of holly
synthetic, probably
latin letters no one knows
polyester gold
rivulets of leading
run glass like black
snow in wheel wells
plaids and knits
fleece and denim
glasses and gold hoops
time's light spills
children carbonate
the clock strikes
we watch the door

*You're My All Creation*

you are the weather
you are the heavens
you are the scarlet sky
that opens summer's eyes

you are the solar spray
on a seaside day
you are the silken sheets
gliding my skin to sleep

fall on me
we'll burst in singularity

you are the quiet snow
the golden city glow
you are my tinsel town
undo that dressing gown

fall on me
we'll burst in singularity
we'll spiral like a galaxy
as preordained as gravity

in Hubble's field
it's you revealed

you're my all creation, honey

## Quantum Entanglement

We swirl in thick pollen.
Cats spring her step. We joke
of creating a Strays 2016
calendar, dub neighborhood
celebs O'Malley or Otter,
send snaps from Cat Town
and Kitty City. At home,
she rocks and swaddles
her pliant, whinging longhair.

Apart, she texts *something
really bad happened today.*
Without elaboration I see
her face bend to rub short,
prickly hair between gold
eyes. I flinch as the tabby
bolts into a passing car's tire.

She later confirmed my account.

## We Will Make No Distinction

*We will make no distinction between the terrorists who committed these acts and those who harbor them.*

- George W. Bush. September 11, 2001

The Sharp Edge bar
in Friendship, Pittsburgh.
70 taps arrayed like crayons
in a jumbo pack. *Delirium
Tremens,* neon signs and pink
elephants in the room. We went
for blanket of murmur and clinking
tableware, wood seats worn soft
as sea glass, sole threat the digestive
implications of cheese sticks or wings.

W bursts all TVs, squints as if reading
too-small type. A laugh brims the bottle
of my throat. *Somebody thinks
this is funny,* a man says.

Sociologists later found mostly rage.
My legs washed out like a sandcastle.
*Your skyline,* said quiet Scot therapist.
*It hits you harder.* American flags
broke out like hives. My chills spiked
when white biplane shadowed sun
of our attic apartment. I called
the FBI. *You'll be alright,* agent said,

her voice cracked as paint on wood
bleachers in an empty park.

*We will make no distinction...*
followed by Christian verse subtle
as neon gang signs. Now the ex-Prez
paints himself naked into a corner,
washes like colors down a bathtub drain.

## Always Sometimes

My son loves streams,
calls them *steam,* says
*sometimes cars are blue
or always.* Always if I'm still
my mind catches tired fears:
soldiers under overpass,
birds and disease. In Paris,
storefront of taxidermied
rats, traps big enough
to catch a Vice President
ditching the sinking ship.
Women and children
last. It's men with gold
watches skipping stairs
to a secretary idling
in a convertible. Wish
my bonds were convertible.
There's a care tag
on every garment, a wide
recall list and sometimes
your car drives to the
emergency room. It's March,
winter always almost over.
Light in the living room
fades. Brownout? Just sun
slipping behind clouds.

## Suspension

My mother mails postcards
of her foundering memory. Midnight,
guest room, nights lately cracked
by cries of sick children. My ex-
girlfriend and I orbit oblong ellipses,
our swirling concoction a substance
best controlled. I wipe vinegar
on doorknobs, powerless as a boy
hurling matchbox cars at a punitive
father. I'm the father fumbling phrase,
touching shoulder to diffuse steam.
                         We have zero
levels of undo. Could a sleepless night
crack me like pint glass in dishwasher's
heat? Equanimity lost like Legos
down a vent lined by glinting pennies.
Optimism slips like fingerings to a song
composed in dream. I hope to settle
like silt from suspension, smile unfiltered.

## *Not About Girls*

*when I was ten I'd BMX for the win
a bitchin' power slide and a mag rim grin*

*later flashlight on a paperback
I'd thrill to cracks in time or galactic attack*

*I'll just go back like Doc
gimmie a gigawatt
she will be soon forgot*

*this song is not about girls*

*I'm at a party and I feel like Spock
caught up in human ways that he cannot grok*

*is her glance a signal sent without a word?
ten anthropologists would take a year to concur*

*or maybe I'm just dumb
so let me suck my thumb
and hum a childish tune*

*this song is not about girls*

*you say some play's the thing
the protagonist doth protest too much, methinks
but I don't want another game
one more mislaid peg and my battleship will sink*

## 1991

New kid in school of banker's sons:
blond bowl cuts, lacrosse sticks.
In plaid shorts and curls, I'm a white
dandelion ripe for mowing. I parse
MTV like code for clues to cool, dream
green visions of Baghdad bombs.
Bully shoves me into urinal. Dad says
*shower, comb your hair.* I fly low, head
in fiction. Blackboard becomes a squint.
First glasses: faceted shock of leaves.

## Portrait of Lazarus

Parishioners boxed mom's
books for her cross-country
jarring. Before her memory
watered, she clasped hands
with tomorrow's dead.
A loss a week in hospice
bled her tears like twisting
a washcloth. Now she tugs
bedcovers from holy trinity
of cats, piano silent, paint
brushes dusting in closet.
She once painted Lazarus
first person as he shocked up
in saturated color. She fades
like a 70's Kodak to tempo
of a distant hymn.

## Remember Who You Are

She is my unmapped mountain village,
pinnacle of snow-bleached beams,
billowing steam, spiced air clear
as if sky didn't exist. Within lodging
softly tendered, bedding curated
like bouquets unfurls, wet boots
forgotten by door. But this village
departs. I circle under lens flares
in rutted snow, brush powder
to unearth a flannel shirt bound
in glinting ribbon. Her handwrit note:
*remember who you are.*

# Driving Jonas to School

*Music day, or quiet?*
*Quiet,* little son says,
low sun diffused through cloud
like a flashlight behind paper.
Yesterday he climbed upstairs
to toddler bed in darkness,
bragged later of stillness:
*I did nothing! I laid there so long!*
He watches big brother Toby
play violin. Twice his size,
Toby breaks waves. Jonas
lets sea foam tickle his toes.
*Do you know the barn owl's*
*predator?* He asks. *Stoats.*
Jonas wrote a pop song of bikes,
travel. In studio, he sang perched
on the edge of a leather couch.
In my arm's crook, he rocked.

## Homecoming

pear tree blossoms burst
at parking garage's edge
clouds pearl the sky

a woman in brown coat
strolls with cigarette
cars roar in matte sun

my wife and sons gone
to Oklahoma. Cats yowl
the house like a vacant gym

return now imminent as children
poised for Easter egg hunt,
bright as Dorothy's first blinks

of Oz. Fear of loss is shade
pulled against joy. Let it rattle
and flap in an open window

*Sneaky*

*by the fire we're making up stories*
*about the couple slow dancing in their forties*
*we're sipping wine unwinding time like tycoons*

*you and I are aromas from a kitchen*
*a slow-cooked meal we don't get to eat*
*now we gotta sift the seasoning from the stew*

*but Sneaky, Sneaky I love you*

*summer drive, odometer rising*
*rolling through the hills, I'm improvising*
*seventeen twists to make the turns take more time*

*at a party you're keeping so quiet*
*alone in a loveseat I'll swing by*
*I'd whisk us both away like a genie if I knew the lines*

*Sneaky, Sneaky please be mine*

*If I misapprehend that I'll love you forever*
*the Dalai Lama can scold us together*
*'cuz our sweaters are brushing arms right now*

*it's been a while I'm starting to miss you*
*yeah a day so I'm making it an issue*
*let's walk to Fric & Frac for a beer*

*Sneaky, Sneaky you're so near*

Political Agenda

pluck mulberries on summer
sidewalks. rinse chlorine
from kids' hair. don't dwell
on the third rail. advocate truth
in bagels. erect lunchroom
pulpits for closet soccer
virtuosos. give figs. sing
to the whites of their eyes.
don't defriend gun nuts
until they hatch, treehugger.

## Goats, Biscuits, Bees

autumn night we wander arm in arm
laugh and cry in our specs
slip off my gloves to touch your tears and we embrace
you softly ask in my neck

can we have goats, biscuits, bees
oh that sounds fine to me
I know you've gotta leave
but we'll have goats, biscuits, bees

you're called to walk the crowd wherever voices shout
you wonder can it be fair
to leave a love to tune and worry to your sound
dear heart, you're already there

can we have goats, biscuits, bees
oh that sounds fine to me
I know you've gotta leave
but we've got goats, biscuits, bees

waves and noise
spinning into space
bring your voice
to me as I age
still sunbeams
coffee in the air
are you home?
I'll meet you there

## Wildlife Observatory

My office overlooks
military cemetery.
Rifle reports, staccato
carnations bursting
like wounds. Black
cars line chain link
fence. I stroll weed-
cracked sidewalk
down under highway
bridge. Muffled torrent
of tires above echoes
like waterfall in cavern.
Colorful tags bloom
from concrete. Two
teens wander high
on gravel bank kicking
stones among glass
and rags. Neon backpacks
peek between columns.
I interlope in dress pants,
sweat brimming the collar
of my body temperature.
I hurry into green heat
of sun and crickets
past the bridge's shade.

## Charlene and Manny

Manny is a *horse,*
says Charlene:
a girl on a farm
at the world's northern corner

She blasts dance pop
from the steps of the cabin
her foster father carved
from his own trees

Manny tramples rows
of freshly sprouted beans,
stares with his milky
eye. Charlene sings along

In summer she'll dip her feet
off the dock 'til they purple.
A black fly crawls her knee,
ball bearing drawing blood

Charlene's foster mother
pours tea in the kitchen,
spots Manny in the beans,
shouts and charges the door

## Raytown Open House

Dead end
in stranger's
two-car garage.
Moldy ducts, AC
off. Garage door
windows yellowed.
Our realtor on tiptoes
pulls the handle,
rifles her key ring.
We spelunk
into beige halls.
Cigarette ash carpet.
No pictures. No art.
Turn a corner: hairy
back of sleeping man,
ceiling fan still.

*Drill To The Hull*

*1am
they took away my girl
she should be nestled
in her covers
the aftermath
broken fan blade spinning
the thick of august heat
sweats the label off my beer*

*I'm on a sinking ship
and I'm the one
with a drill to the hull*

*I reach at night
I find an empty bed
murmurs carry
from your study
in the morning you'll
sunshine her facts again
I kneel on slippered feet
with an ear upon your door*

*I'm on a sinking ship
and I'm the one
with a drill to the hull*

*I'll play my turn
a hand that's full of nothing
every move
is sure to damage something
the ocean churns
the cliffs ahead are listing
the wheel won't turn
now it's time*

*Monday drive, I'm burning down to fumes
metal beetles snake for miles
in the forecast it's all record highs again
the gassing asphalt snugs
the tie around my neck*

Forecast

a procession
of angry orange
suns my son
bawling I carry
him out break
his anger
like a fever
he rubs and smells
basil leaves
picks and mouths
mint crushed
and spat in heat
yard is good
for looking
not loitering
catalpa arches up
leaves fending off sun
like green hands
we planted catalpa
after silverleaf fell
when silver-haired man
hauled dead tree
for lowest price
chopped and hunched
each stout piece
gripped bark
bare handed
as he wilted
sweat-slicked
near his sweltering
black flatbed

### The Art Teacher

My grandmother hit
crossing with art supplies
by driver who saw a bag.
The wall phone's ring,
my mother's unnatural
silence. Handset clunked
back to cradle, the bell
sounded anew: my father
announcing my sister's
birth. My grandmother,
skinny gray paintbrush,
favored still lifes, wood
spinning wheel dusting
by the dining table.
She'd heat my favorite
canned soup for lunch.
In summer, I'd climb cool
brick kiln in her backyard.

## Statue of Limitations

Mike squats barefoot
on the stoop, humming
to thunder of summer's
first storm. Smoke rings

curl from his pursed mouth
like clouds above a seaside
of darts and roller coasters,
sugar cones in sand.

In California, his girlfriend
counts weeks in chalk.
He seals an application
for a position in Texas.

He leaves in green twilight.
Soft rain slowly washes
the diesel sheen of his scuffed
hatchback from the street.

## Seacats

Driving to work
to plainclothes singing
of a band I've never heard.
Songs of expectations
colliding like pool balls,
couples dropping like thuds
in corner pockets or snap,
crack and ricochet, leaving
bodies the size of planets
blocking the next shot.
It's the energy of the break:
spin, chalk or scratched felt.
Slouching man on a stool
where your cue should be.

## Prophet and Loss

My brain's a jerky
transmission: expense
ratios, three five seven-year
returns. Squeak a digital
dime. Either way I drive, burn
polar bear pelts, chew straws
in water glasses. I'm up
for whatever: contemporary
fiction book club, ten
thousand beer-hours
of peak pontificating,
Japanese cat collecting.
My checkbox life: home,
office, home office.
My marriage's best hours
spent asleep. Parenting
in ten-minute increments,
attention an Exacto. Balsa
jets crack like matzoh
to rocks if lofted from porch
of seaside hotel. Adulthood
calls us in for dinner. Pass
the bitter herbs.

## Betty Moody's Cave

Star Island, Isles of Shoals
an hour of turquoise chop via ferry.
Sun whitewashes sight for miles.
My little brother, father and I step
quietly, sneakers gripping pocked,
bleached rocks. Tiny flowers, shallow
roots. Deadly nightshade I've heard,
but can't tell. Near seagull nests, Dad
carries a thick stick. The gulls circle,
strafing like lightning to the roof
of the hotel of graying, brittle wood
capping the island, burnt twice to embers.
Under dappled clouds, the mouth
of Betty Moody's cave is cool, still.
My father lifts and lowers my brother,
too small to jump. By legend, Betty fled
here with her kids, cowering as natives
scoured the island purging colonizers.
Hearing screams, smelling smoke,
her daughter cried. Betty surged,
smothering the girl as natives passed.
Sudden stillness in Betty's arms
sucked all sound. Rising from rock,
she walked off island's edge to merge
with sea, clutching the stone
of her daughter.

Today, the cave muffles
only gulls. My brother kicks his feet.
Above, black boulders burst surf.
Each morning, my brother rises
for Polar Bear Club, leaps into icy
saltwater that sucks his warmth
like a vacuum vanishing sand.

## I Need You To Be Real

walked the block alone tonight
in the side of my sight
I still pass you

my sky is dust and Mars
I don't know where you are
so I'll ask you

cold air cut with grief
too thin to breathe
I can't grasp you

shards of a final scene
furrowed into me
oh my Matthew

can't take that you're a story
I need you to be real

our home a dusty shrine
only creaks are mine
brittle flowers

you taught me how to swim
I'm foundering
at this hour

*out front we'd set the sun*
*loveseat for one*
*can I face this?*

*carve M into the floor*
*by the kitchen door*
*can't erase us*

*can't take that you're a story*
*I need you to be real*

*I don't ask why you died*
*there's just no reason for the way things go*
*hopes turn and cars collide*
*who am I to be now I cannot know*

## Christmas Day

sidewalks glazed
furrows of ice

only liquor store open
no traffic on 39th

pale blue pickup
tailpipe steaming

fingers fist for feeling
nostrils freeze

at home, kids trundle
meadow of torn paper

Christmases past, my family
caroled: clarinet, piano

stepmother singing
now between us miles

of wind.
      I'll call. They'll pass

me around, forget ages
we'll pretend the phone spools

enough yarn for knitting
in mirror I'll worry my hair

patchy as snow
in brown grass

## Mantoloking Redux

I summon old selves
by singing old songs.
Like walking an apartment
long turned over, boxes
ushered down creaking
steps. The lyrics read
as relevant as my teenage
journals on nightmares
whose villains (fried egg
of drug addiction) strike
poses preposterous as '50s
Superman foes. I sink
into my old voice like worn
flannel vs. slim-fit dress shirt.

I've lost tracks, trashed
the wrong files. Can't undo
photos flood plastered
to a basement floor.

Today's black mailbox
lolls a 1960's Thank You
card: slinky, arch cartoon
cat à la I Dream of Jeannie.
I lay the card in an earth-brown
box, lie on my earth-brown
couch to trace my grandmother's
thin collection of writings.

Odes to cats and girlhood
anecdotes transfix her flapper
social-worker self poorly
as paintings twisted edgewise
at thirty feet. Nearby, two time
capsules read The Tick
and press puzzle edges,
respectively, prepping
the course for the table
where I'll be cleared.

# Ends

*An end should be sad,*
he says. Oval glasses,
lawn chair. Yes, or the meal
was unseasoned. Pop Tart,
no filling. All bass passed
from the mix. Ends sometimes
aren't. A turnpike exit missed.
An invitation washed insincere
by rain of no replies.

Never count your chickens:
year upon year dubbed
on warbly cassette until
tape's tangle yanked free.

Aversion to ends is allergy
to air: impractical. Unbearable
pain is borne. *That's not
what you do when you get hit.*

When to not upright the bike
from skinned knees?

When to savor appetite's
salty dissolve?

## Stuck Spark

Clogged left ear,
world's mix cockeyed.
Days brew thin like tea
in lukewarm water.
Sex comes in streams.
Statecraft now reality TV,
fraud priced in every vote.
Even cauliflower is broccoli's
soft spoken, underachieving cousin.
I am windless white dandelion,
spark stuck between poles.

*She's The Memory You Keep*

*when you chase for novelty
prep a page for tragedy
lens flare of a city night
freight train coming on your right
at speed with her on your arm
she blooms under all your charms
as you glide try not to think
of the ice underneath your feet*

*salt of tears
painted dawn
bitter tea
you'll carry on
take a run
get some sleep
she's the memory you keep*

*to a song you seemed to know
love rose like a sourdough
a loom was soon entwined
she'd call late and you didn't mind
the days got short and cold
twilight by the time you're home
her note flapping on your door
your love has flown its course*

*salt of tears*
*painted dawn*
*bitter tea*
*you'll carry on*
*take a run*
*get some sleep*
*she's the memory you keep*

*at lakeside under a roiling sky*
*your bodies blurring in the night*
*you'll love her until the day you die*

*far away the crying's done*
*pale shore under whitewash sun*
*dip your toes in the cloudy bay*
*too cold to swim today*
*phone streaked with salt and sand*
*her name that you tap to send*
*not sure you can take what's next*
*as you wait for her to text*

# Silt

*The game, kids, is to keep the water
away* said the chimney sweep. Niagara
will carry casinos over its rim. Even barnacles
can't cut like water, despite the burning
of my bloody foot. The Grand Canyon
is a deepening wound. My thumb splits in winter.
Sea glass is softness of my grandmother's
fading vision. Ice breakers — real Russian
ones — rise up, smash down, shatter like vodka
on my father. We call three-foot icicles looming
off gutters *child killers*. Hailstones litter
torn daffodil carnage like spilled innards
of a three-hole punch. Even rock salt residue
curves like sandbar squelching between my toes.

# 84 WPM

*I am an excellent*
*typing machine*
I say to the back
of the receptionist
at the temp agency

Wrapped in smooth
gray suit on tiptoe
hanging streamers,
she reminds me
of an unrequited crush
from high school French
named Marjorie,
spiced jam for kings

*I am an excellent*
*typing machine*
I say again

She steps down,
gathers clipboard,
asks for two forms
of identification

## 40 Days, 40 Nights

The plane leapt to and fro
like toddler thrashing temper.
Touchdown, gentle bobbing
of landing gear depressurized
all like Thanksgiving served.
I arrived, hotel kitchen closed,
but night manager thawed
bread. *Storms tomorrow?*
I asked. Said she: *I'm hearing
40 days, 40 nights.* Sunset sea
swept my feet a salty kiss.
Snapped balcony selfie to prove
my life. That night rain drummed
the window of my beating heart.
Days later I flew, arrived with dry
certainty like a multiplication table.
I smelled slush, taxi's leather seats,
damp leaves mouldering the curb.

## Quick Cuts

My son sleepwalking:
naked howls of pain.
*What hurts?* I ask.
*Me,* he says.

Obama's premature
peace prize. Debating
Kill List by conference
call in windowless room.

My marriage wobbles
like a gyroscope.
I tap it gently
with my ring finger.

Reading Bradbury.
Rockets and clear
threats. Marching doom
of ourselves.

## After the Inauguration

Joy flooded storm
drains like juice clenched
from every lemon,
curdled from corrugated
pipe into fetid rivers
skimmed with sheen
of deregulated cat food
factories. Hope flew
like swallows to nest
beneath bridge girders,
shivering unseen below
semis. Punxsutawney Phil
shrieked from the tower's
looming shadow, heralding
four years without sun.
Upon the slope of volcanic
ash, pink geraniums burst
ripe with anticipation.

# Burrs

left waitress
card game
on credit card skid

yuca comforts
like boiled potatoes
in Thanksgiving butter

purple potato sunset
out car window
unseasonable warmth

seasonal. solar
voltage cranks motor
of bedroom air filter

bought a straw
for sucking puddles
and river water

framed insurance policy
above the mantle
coworker killed himself

over breakfast cereal
last panel
of his graphic novel

## Mid-American Shakespeare

For her, I had Antony's madness,
multi-lane swerves to drive
highways wrong way. Switched
to Dvorak and unlearned to type.
Bashed sonnets with my palms.
Founded a chickpea delivery service.
Wound myself 'til the strings
popped. It's my script: no blinding
bolt of Shakespearean talent.
No stabbings or saboteur nymphs.
I maintain plausible deniability,
redact all thumb bites and roses.
Don't worry, honey. My run ends
unseen.

# Prospectus

"A" scale scratches
on preschooler's bow.
Weaning myself from texts
to a woman with no time
for undirected conjugation.
I craft life plans like brochures
for sunken islands. My plan's
a glove box of used Chipotle
napkins and dead flashlight
batteries. Let's partner, accrue
equity in milk cartons, sow
sorrell sour as pale clover
in shade of youth's duplex.

## Art of Not Asking

If I was a half-naked piano-
pounding woman brimming
like an over-poured milkshake
with legitimacy and horsepower,
I wouldn't woo with Scrabble.
In college, I etched tendonitis
in my wrists until a miniature
Egyptian doctor gestured *don't flex
the electrodes*. A taller ex joked
I should wear platforms. I'm so smart.
99th percentile Iowa Basic Skills.
Six me's on every street sautéing
kale. Daily I tap lbs into my phone,
charting my singular collapse
to two dimensions. Fifteen-year
career, ten-mile commute,
This American Life, standing
desk. My feet plant in a slick bed
of kidney stones.

*I Do Or Adieu*

*all my life*
*is folding to this minute*
*in your pretty hands*

*with this box*
*I harbor in my pocket*
*like a secret plan*

*when we drink*
*we teeter near the topic*
*but you change the tune*

*now your glass of wine*
*is streaked with empty*
*I'm running outta soon*

*"I do" or "adieu"*
*I need "I do" or "adieu"*

*took a walk alone*
*as the sidewalk simmered*
*on that balmy night*

*in this urban orb*
*churning on and ever*
*we're just fireflies*

*"I do" or "adieu"*
*I need "I do" or "adieu"*

*your dress blinding white*
*like a seaside in July*
*pictures burning in my mind's eye*

# Forgiveness

elusive as a single cork
stoppering a wine geyser
in a roadside wheat field

unexpected as a shining
coat of blue paint under
wallpaper you scraped

sudden as a cymbal crash
tossed from the roof
of an ivy-covered garage

complete as the saturation
of a bathrobe at the bottom
of summer's swimming pool

*Like Petrichor*

*your home is glowing twilight gray*
*our knees are touching to your delicate wordplay*

*kisses come in little rounds*
*you say your roommate won't be bothered by our sound*

*we could have some fun 'ere monday pulls*
*the curtain of the night down from the sun*
*such a pretty one*

*you can stay*
*I wanna go to bed*

*curling fingers conjure thirst*
*as you clutch me we bear down until we burst*

*scent and sweat now intertwined*
*got your glasses on you can try on mine*
*are we out of time?*

*you can stay*
*I wanna go to bed*

*like petrichor*
*from a summer storm*
*you're soft and warm*

## Anniversary

When opened, car's glove
box wafts your perfume.
Hours of repartee minced
into garlic of Facebook sarcasm.
Smiley face.
               I know your Julian
number, password, shoulder click,
scent of nape, how your face
softens in dark.
               Bar. I watch honky tonk
haunted by your judgement. That night,
phantom physician, you place
my arms at my side.

## B7

Sliding doors part.
You meander
with silver current
of baggage claim:
red plaid scarf,
cat eye glasses.

We smile, don't hug.
You tuck my sweater
tag against my neck.

I roll your bag to garage
as you spill Christmas tales
of cousins, uncles, aunts.
How you toed over your mother's
tripwires by arriving mid-meal
blanketed by conversation.

Southbound skyline glitters.
*Beautiful,* you say, reshelving
our 'burgh with more elegant
literature.
        We drink gose perched
on barstools, talk of our fumbling
for each other through deeds,
words and reports: I fed the cat
your boyfriend didn't. The man

you say needs therapy, who set
my table once, saying little.

You sign the check in thanks
for the ride.

The ballpoint stutters
as I define privilege.

## Once in a Lifetime

My heart is a kettle
rustling on her blue
flame. We roll over
Sunday hills, coffee
in our hands, Once
In a Lifetime soft
on the stereo.

After ice cream,
I hold words so loud
I can't hear her story.
Driving her back, I lurch
for a man suddenly seen:
her sharp inhalation.

In her driveway, I burble
my confession. *Stop
crying!* she smiles,
*We have everything.
You just can't put
your dick in me.*

Jesse Kates is the songwriter, singer and guitarist
behind The Sexy Accident.

The songs in Extra Pith can be heard on *Champagne Babycakes,*
the world's first card game pop album.

Recordings by The Sexy Accident

*Champagne Babycakes*
*Lavender 3*
*Ninja Ninja Fight Darth Vader*
*You're Not Alone*
*Now That She's Gone*
*A Merry Christmas To You*
*Mantoloking*
*Kinda Like Fireworks*
*Tourism*

visit sexyaccident.com

www.ingramcontent.com/pod-product-compliance
Lightning Source LLC
Chambersburg PA
CBHW021448080526
44588CB00009B/744